D1353499

# BLACK ROADS

## THE FAMINE IN IRISH LITERATURE

ROBERT SMART

This essay is part of the interdisciplinary series *Famine Folios*,
covering many aspects of the Great Hunger in Ireland from 1845-52.

# CONTENTS

An Gorta Mór

LUCAN
LIBRARY
TEN 62 16/22

**Figure 1** | Daniel Macdonald, *An Irish Peasant Family Discovering the Blight of their Store*

# INTRODUCTION

We sometimes forget that Ireland's literature includes a long famine narrative that reaches farther back than the Great Famine of 1845. Crop failure and privation, famine and its physical and cultural destruction, have long been prominent tropes in Irish literature in both the Irish and English languages. This is likely the only national literature where this is true. The question, then, is not simply how *An Gorta Mór* ("the Great Hunger") changed Irish literature, but rather how the terrors of the 1845 Famine altered this long narrative about famine in Ireland. What also seems clear is that the experience of *An Gorta Mór* refracted earlier work about famine and provided writers after 1852 with a powerful metaphor for Ireland's long colonial struggle.

Before 1845, famine in Irish language poetry, for example, addressed God about the failure of the potato crop:

> *It is not war or continual strife between great kings*
>
> *Nor a storm at sea wreaking havoc on shipping*
>
> *Nor the sound of arms being sharpened for battle*
>
> *That has caused the wailing of the men of Ireland, their children and wives.*
>
> *But the war of the [potato] plots that were demolished and dissolved*
>
> *The civil war that took the potato from us*
>
> *This war of the frost waged by God on us*
>
> *This is the war they most deplore and that they most widely lament continually*
>
> (qtd. in Ó Gráda and Ó Muirithe 54).

There is epistemological certainty in this rendering: one kind of strife gives way to another – God wages war through nature, frosts, crop failures, the burial of the dead. And periodically, God wars against his people, who then have to make amends. After the Great Hunger, there is no clear historical context for understanding the scale of the suffering and the cultural destruction that followed it. This epistemological puzzlement becomes a persistent trope in Famine writing.

As Luke Gibbons noted in his essay in this Famine Folio series, *Limits of the Visible: Representing the Great Hunger*, there are no actual photographs of famine-stricken areas of the country or of famine victims. In the images that accompanied narrative reporting between 1845 and 1850, such as the artwork of James Mahony for *The Illustrated London News* (*ILN*), "there is no depiction of the hideous scenes described in print that haunted future generations: people eating grass with green-stained mouths, dogs digging up cadavers, bodies buried like refuse in mass graves" (12). It is, Gibbons rightly notes, "as if words could go into places where images fear to tread" (15). Mahony's images are more suggestive than depictive: we see abandoned habitations or stand outside a "fever cabin" while a neighbor looks in. We are left to imagine what is hidden from our eyes.

For this essay, then, the depictive power of realistic literature – as well as of contemporary paintings that address the Famine and its consequences – depends upon two idiosyncratic interpretive contexts, each "*relational*, bound up with what is brought to an image as well as what is brought away from it" (Gibbons 29). We tend to rely on what we have seen or known before to help us understand the new, and that habit of mind naturally restricts our ability to really "see" things which are outside the boundaries of what we have already experienced. Furthermore, the "meaning of things" is almost never in the text; rather, we bring meaning to texts and make them fit the contours of our understanding.[1]

So often during the Famine, the expected signification of scenes of human suffering and duress conflicted with the enormity of what reporters saw. These tectonic misalignments as to the meaning of Famine suffering are often marked by empty village scenes – absences really – or distorted human figures showing the body in extremis, and reliance on a Gothic lexicon of excess and monstrosity. Gibbons was right to rely on Gothic language and imagery in the passages quoted earlier: the Gothic became the only narrative mode that could truly capture the realities of the Famine's destruction. Even in a painting from the period of the Famine like Daniel Macdonald's *An Irish Peasant Family Discovering the Blight of their Store* (1847) (National Folklore Collection, University College Dublin), the arrangement of figures around the blighted stock of potatoes follows compositional convention – the baby at left, next to an innocent and unknowing child, and the patriarch at the center of the human pyramid, flanked by figures looking off into the distance, none of them emaciated or wasted like actual Famine victims **[Figure 1]**. In this and other paintings of the period, the Famine is often "hidden" from view, as in James Mahony's journalistic illustrations **[Figure 2]**. Literature about the Famine would need to tell something closer to the realities of this modern calamity.

**Figure 2** | James Mahony, "The Hut or Watch-House in the Old Chapel Yard" (*ILN*, February 12, 1847) [Detail]

THE HUT OR WATCH-HOUSE IN THE OLD CHAPEL YARD.

# BLACK ROADS

In his novel *The Black Prophet* – which provides the title for this folio – William Carleton intentionally fashions out of the memory of previous famines a powerful literary and political metaphor for the Famine in 1847:

*Having witnessed, last season, the partial, and in this the general failure of the potato crop, he [Carleton] anticipated, as every man must, the fearful visitation which is now almost decimating our wretched population; and it occurred to him that a narrative founded upon it, or, at all events, exhibiting, through the medium of fiction, an authentic detail of all that our unhappy and neglected country has suffered, during past privations of a similar kind, might be calculated to awaken those who legislate for us into something like a humane perception of a calamity that has been almost perennial in the country* (Preface, n. pag.).[2]

Carleton's novel helped change the face and function of famine description in Irish literature. No longer about one famine alone, *The Black Prophet* inaugurated a new discourse in which *An Gorta Mór* represents the depravations of Ireland's contested history. In this way the novel transcends the particular moment of the Great Famine, deploying a lengthy series of famines and privations to stake a claim on English relief for the stricken country.

Carleton was not alone in writing in 1848 from the cultural epicenter of what would become the Great Hunger. James Clarence Mangan, one of the few major Catholic writers to address the Great Famine, directly aligned his experience of famine horrors with Ireland's Gothic tradition [Figure 3]. This was fateful because the Gothic would become a key means of addressing the terrors of 1845-52 from behind an official silence about the Famine that lasted until the middle of the twentieth century.

This literary amalgam was driven by Mangan's sense of tragic doom, something he explores in his unfinished *Autobiography*: "A ruined soul in a wasted frame: the very *idea* and perfection of moral and physical evil combined in one individual" (23). It's in his poetry, however, that Mangan's sense of the Famine as a personal and cultural watershed becomes clear, especially in "The Nameless One" and "Siberia." "The

Nameless One" blends the personal and the observed, referencing Mangan's lethal alcoholism – "The gulf and grave of Maginn and Burns" (5) – and the walking dead left by fever and depravation – "And tell how trampled, derided, hated, / And worn by weakness, disease, and wrong" (8-9). In "Siberia," the transposition of human suffering to an exotic locale – Siberia – does little to mitigate the spoiling of land and people as a result of the potato crop failure and the British failure to provide adequate relief. Post-Famine, the mention of any desolate, wasted landscape in any Irish text becomes a Famine reference, an indication of how powerful this moment in modern Irish history became.

**Figure 3** | Frederic William Burton, *James Clarence Mangan (1803-1849), Poet, after his Death in the Meath Hospital, Dublin, 1849*

A third voice from 1848 addressed the ravages of the Famine from a determinedly political perspective: John Mitchel, who in *Jail Journal* framed the destruction of Georgian Ireland in immediate terms – placing the reader in the middle of death and destruction, as a means of resistance against the closure that traditional mimetic/realistic narratives impose on such events. Mitchel's aim is political: to paint the British response as yet another perfidy visited upon its unfortunate colony. But note that here, as well, the Gothic register serves his aims. The descriptions from Mitchel's account could be taken from anything written by Charles Maturin (Melmoth the Wanderer) or Sheridan Le Fanu (Carmilla): "There is a horrible silence; grass grows before the doors; we fear to look into any door, though they are all open or off the hinges; for we fear to see yellow chapless skeletons grinning there" (416). The scale of devastation in these descriptions is monstrous and so lends itself easily to the appearance of Gothic revenants. [3]

Two things are important to consider. First, of the three narrative modalities established about the Famine by 1848-9 (metaphoric, Gothic, Gothic-political), only one persists beyond the evictions, the death and dying, and the forced emigrations to Canada and the US: the Gothic. There are two reasons for this. After the Famine – undoubtedly the most Gothic event in Irish history – the Gothic became the only narrative form that would allow writers to name the unnameable, to speak of the horrors of that half-decade when historians and novelists had lapsed into silence. Novelists like Anthony Trollope (*Castle Richmond*) relied on the Victorian realistic narrative to cast these events into the background of the story, [4] while post-Famine historians simply dealt with the bare facts of the period. The Famine created a new, distinctly *Irish* Gothic, different from what Ireland's Gothic writers had written previously and also different from English Gothic literature. Once the fictional landscapes and revenants of the Gothic genre had been made real, and once the outlandish plots of these romances had been outdone by the horrors of Famine suffering and death, the Gothic genre in Ireland took on a different epistemology, one that persists into our own century. In these post-Famine texts, "Gothic" refers to both content and modality.

The second important consideration, argued perhaps most notably by Kevin Whelan, runs thusly: representing the "hollowing out of Irish culture" (62), and what are intrinsically Irish sufferings, in English – the language of the colonial power that failed the colony so completely – creates a powerful conundrum. In response to this problem, Irish writers used the English language differently than their British counterparts, thereby inaugurating Ireland's long history of experimental, modernistic prose work that allowed the experience of the colonized to appear between the lines of the colonizer's language, "to allow use of the English language while escaping the specific gravities of its traditions, the dense weight of its parochialisms" (Whelan 62).

Thus, the main literary modes for representing a post-Famine Ireland were the Gothic – as practiced by Anglo-Irish writers like Sheridan Le Fanu and Bram Stoker – and modernist, for the next generation. This division dominates writing about the Famine through most of the twentieth century and persists into the twenty-first, and makes the Famine an important catalyst for both Irish modernism and Irish Gothic. There are even links to American literature, something alluded to in Jock McFadyen's *Irish Gothic* (1987) (Wolverhampton Art Gallery) **[Figure 4]**, a provocative refashioning of Grant Wood's iconic *American Gothic* painting from 1930 which depicts the hidden horrors of rural farm life in America's Midwest. In the case of American literature, it was Charles Brockden Brown, in his novel *Edgar Huntly* (1799), who first wove Irish politics and history into America's Gothic narrative.

Thus, it's fair to speak about post-Famine Irish Gothic literature as distinguishable from that written before the Famine. Before the Famine, work by Charles Robert Maturin, for example *Melmoth the Wanderer* (1820), followed a formula first attributed to Horace Walpole in *The Castle of Otranto* (1765), with some additions

**Figure 4** | Jock McFadyen, *Irish Gothic*

from the Scottish Romance tradition. A strong anti-Catholic narrative set in suspect Catholic terrain is required, with frequent recourse to local legends ("The Bleeding Nun" in Matthew Lewis' *The Monk* (1799), for example), and the stories delivered titillating dangers and narrow rescues with few surprises. After the Famine, the Gothic acquired an ontological menace that G. Richard Thompson describes as "heightened psychological and philosophical perplexity – so much so that such works may be considered not only as uncertain metaphysical texts, but fundamentally as epistemological texts" (27-28). This last point is significant, for therein lies the crucial role of the Gothic as a literary register suitable for representing Famine experiences outside the "legitimate" narratives available within the colony. [5] While pre-Famine Gothic literature is dominated by doomed romantic solitaries whose fates are sealed by hidden curses, post-Famine Gothic literature is dominated by the vampire, that revenant redolent of the all-encompassing colonial power exercised by Britain in response to the Famine.

Ironically, the vampire figure had been introduced to the Anglo-Irish dialogue by the British, who used it to symbolize the parasitical nature of the Irish, a tactic which is typical of colonizing cultures who seek to dehumanize those whom they control economically and culturally. This characterization plagued Irish and English relations throughout the Famine, leading to "relief fatigue" among the English public, and to the adoption of tepid half-measures of relief that merely postponed the inevitable rather than addressing the plight of millions without food. "Two Species of Irish Vampire" by Robert Seymour (1831) (The Victoria and Albert Museum) powerfully evokes British feeling at the time: the unclothed female body (Ireland) is preyed on from across the water by an "absentee" landlord, while the other, a "Law Priest," feeds close at hand from the throat of the prostrate figure **[Figure 5]**. On the tree to the right is noted one of the effects of this ravishing – "Famine" – while a famine figure falls to the left of the unfortunate victim. After the Great Hunger, the figure of the vampire would be deployed by the Irish against the British.

Other Gothic images were attached to the Irish Catholic: Frankenstein's monster, Devil-Fish, Werewolves, the entire pantheon of Gothic revenants illustrated Anglo-Irish fear of the aggrieved Catholic population post-Famine, even though this large majority was mostly unable to read English texts. The most emblematic Irish Gothic novel of the age, *Dracula*, depicts the vampire count as an invader – a colonizer, ironically enough – who seeks to breach the center of the British Empire, London. A closer reading of the novel, however, reveals some anomalies that belie the surface narrative. The two female leads, Mina Murray and Lucy Westenra, are Irish and orphaned, and many descriptions of Dracula's homeland of Transylvania strongly resemble eyewitness accounts of the Famine and the ravages it brought the West and South of Ireland. As with most colonial/post-colonial dialogues, the "ease with which colonial Gothic could be turned against itself" (Gibbon 82) led to a redeployment of the vampire figure as a depiction of English rapacity in this centuries-old colonial relationship. An example of this reversal is shown in John D. Reigh's illustration

"Ireland Wrestles with Famine While Mr. Balfour Plays Golf" (1890) (*United Ireland*, August 23, 1890) **[Figure 6]**.

Stoker is himself an interesting personality at this transition. He was born in 1847 ("Black '47") in Clontarf, and was such a weak child that he did not walk until nearly seven. During his sickness, his mother Charlotte told him stories of the 1832-3 cholera epidemic, and later in life he rather inexplicably spoke of himself as a famine victim. His first novel, *The Snake's Pass* (1890) should be considered a post-Famine work: in it he imagines Ireland as a "proper colony" which has been converted from an undeveloped, primitive island into an industrial paradise, presided over by an Englishman – Arthur Severin – and his young Irish colleen, Nora Joyce. This transformation had long been a hope of English politicians, and many saw the Famine as the Providential tool to accomplish it. The real Gothic masterpiece post-Famine, however, is *Dracula* (1897).

*Dracula's* importance lies in its adoption of a modernist aesthetic. If we take Kevin Whelan's point that the rise of Irish modernism is due largely to post-Famine Irish writers "turning linguistic disenfranchisement to advantage, enlarging rather than contracting its possibilities" (62), then the problematic ending of Stoker's masterpiece makes epistemological sense. The original ending of the novel was conventional: the sky and the earth conspire to destroy Dracula's castle and swallow it in a volcanic inferno. Shortly before the novel was printed, Stoker carefully excised this ending and substituted for it a post scriptum in which the vampire hunters – seven years after the demise of the Count – revisit the narrative and chronology that

Mina (Murray) Harker crafted to box-in and destroy the vampire count. Instead of a coherent narrative, Harker and Van Helsing discover that all they have is sheets of paper, "nothing but a mass of typewriting" (418). This "Note" at the end of the novel invites us to read through the story to its post-colonial subtext in which the Famine dimensions of the novel become clear. While the Famine and its aftermath are largely absent from historical narratives, the Famine survives in Stoker's modernist Gothic masterpiece.

One final point on the Gothic: even though writers like Le Fanu and Stoker were discouraged from setting their tales in Ireland (by publishers like J. M. Bentley and Sons in London), the landscapes in the tales were clearly Irish, from Le Fanu's Styria to Stoker's Transylvania. English audiences had long been educated into seeing Ireland as an exotic, backward land of monsters and marvels and so "rereading" these novels as Irish was uncomplicated. Moreover, readers of reports about Famine-ravaged areas of Ireland imagined them as real Gothic landscapes: skeletons, graves, body parts, the deformed living looking more like the dead, down to that grim symbol of the workhouse and its adjacent mass grave.

Figure 6 | John D. Reigh, "Ireland Wrestles with Famine While Mr. Balfour Plays Golf" (*United Ireland*, August 23, 1890)

**Figure 7** | Harry Clarke, *"The Dreamers" by Lennox Robinson and "The Countess Cathleen" by W. B. Yeats*

When Bram Stoker retired to his St. George's Square home in London, the age belonged to the Irish modernists: James Joyce, W. B. Yeats and Samuel Beckett. In his landmark *Writing the Irish Famine*, Chris Morash noted that "absence" is the distinctive feature of Irish writing after the Famine, and the chief architect of stage absence and silence is Samuel Beckett. However, the most directly engaged with the Famine of this triumvirate was Yeats. While his controversial verse play *Countess Cathleen* (1912) reproduces imagery from the more gruesome Famine narratives ("Two nights ago, at Carrick-orus churchyard, / A herdsman met a man who had no mouth, / Nor eyes, nor ears; his face a wall of flesh" [9-12]), the play's inspiration grows from Yeats's interest in a nebulous Gaelic mythology that preceded English colonization. It was not so much the terrors of that period that concerned Yeats, Lady Augusta Gregory and company per se, but the opportunity offered by the Famine to writers and poets to mine this pre-conquest mythology (even if they had to invent it). As Seamus Deane has noted in *Strange Country: Modernity and Nationhood in Irish Writing since 1790* (1997), writers of the Irish Literary Revival achieved "the remarkable feat of ignoring the Famine and rerouting the claim for cultural exceptionalism through legend rather than through history" (110). The "hollowed-out culture" mentioned earlier provided transit to an imagined culture while ignoring the actual culture that perished between 1845 and 1852. The beatific ending of *Countess Cathleen*, after she has sacrificed her life for the starving peasants on her estate – as illustrated by Harry Clarke in the famous Geneva Window – highlights this point, and her final words reflect the mythological locus of the play **[Figure 7]**. Yeats' countryman Joyce, however, had no interest in the Fianna and faeries of the imagined country of the Irish Literary Revival, and held his older contemporary in slight contempt for being "too old" **[Figures 8 and 9]**.

The signal work from Joyce's *Dubliners* for this topic is "The Dead." For many critics, the later addition of "The Dead" to the collection marks Joyce's development to aesthetic maturity. Representing Dublin as a collection of "dead" citizens caught

**Figure 8** | John Butler Yeats, *Portrait of William Butler Yeats (1865-1939), Poet*

by the "nets" of politics, church, and history speaks to what Yeats's work would not: the graveyard silence of a country devastated by a catastrophe largely unacknowledged by both writers and historians. Specifically, "The Dead" deals with displacement: Gabriel Conroy's displacement from his native country and culture, Gretta's displacement from her Galway past and the lover who died there, and the displacement of the other guests from any meaningful future. This is especially true of Gabriel's two aunts, one of whom is most likely close to dying (as we learn in *Ulysses*), and the other who is fading away into a past she struggles to remember. The nationalism of Miss Ivors, who accuses Gabriel of being a "West Briton," sounds rather tinny in the company of the other dinner guests, and forces her into an early departure before dinner.

The part of the story that most clearly represents the Famine comes toward the end, as Gabriel and Gretta drive to the Gresham Hotel where Gabriel wishes to make love to his wife. Until now, everything – including Gabriel's fretful delivery of the dinner speech – has noted the passing of all things, even those gathered around the table. Instead of a successful seduction, Gabriel listens to Gretta's tearful recollection of Michael Furey's wooing and dying for her. After Gretta finishes her story and falls asleep, Gabriel realizes that she has known real love and he has not, and then the tale concludes with a Famine scene:

*A few light taps upon the pane made him turn to the window. It had begun to snow again. He watched sleepily the flakes, silver and dark, falling obliquely against the lamplight. The time had come for him to set out on his journey westward. Yes, the newspapers were right: snow was general all over Ireland. It was falling on every part of the dark central plain, on the treeless hills, falling softly upon the Bog of Allen and, farther westward, softly falling into the dark mutinous Shannon waves. It was falling, too, upon every part of the lonely churchyard on the hill where Michael Furey lay buried. It lay thickly drifted on the crooked crosses and headstones, on the spears of the little gate, on the barren thorns. His soul swooned slowly as he heard the snow falling faintly through the universe and faintly falling, like the descent of their last end, upon all the living and the dead* (223-4).

We have left Gabriel's Dublin here and returned to 1845-1852 in the west of Ireland; the scene is a revelation, an unveiling in which the "dead" figures and metropolis of 1904 are transcended by the cultural tailings of the destruction that followed the Famine. While the Famine might have disappeared entirely from public discourse, Joyce shows it to be as present in Irish cultural life as it was during the "Black '47."

Perhaps the best starting point for any discussion of the presence of the Famine in Joyce's modernist masterpiece *Ulysses* is Seamus Deane's observation:

*The historical debate about nationalism and colonialism, which is also a debate about modernity and atrocity, of which the contemporary version known as revisionism is a reprise, begins with the Famine. It is a debate generated by the question of what the Famine meant* ("Dumbness and Eloquence" 110).

**Figure 9** | Jacques-Emile Blanche, *James Joyce*

For Irish modernism, of which *Ulysses* is the exemplar, the Famine is the epistemological starting point. Leopold Bloom travels the city of Dublin with a potato in his pocket which reminds him of small betrayals during the day: his cuckolding by Blazes Boylan, being attacked by "the Citizen" (based on Michael Cusack, founder of the Gaelic Athletic Association) for being Jewish, anti-semitic slights from nearly everyone in his circle. More importantly, it keeps the Famine close to the surface of the narrative, even if it is referred to only twice by Bloom: once as he contemplates the beastly eating habits of his fellow Dubliners, and again as he briefly considers the compounded history of the Famine in response to the bloated patriotism of "the Citizen" in the "Cyclops" episode of the novel. Bloom muses:

*They were driven out of house and home in the black 47. Their mudcabins and their shielings by the roadside were laid low by the batteringram and the Times rubbed its hands and told the whitelivered Saxons there would soon be as few Irish in Ireland as redskins in America. Even the grand Turk sent us his piasters. But the Sassenach tried to starve the nation at home while the land was full of crops that the British hyenas bought and sold in Rio de Janeiro. Ay, they drove out the peasants in hoards. Twenty thousand of them died in the coffinships* (324).

It is important that Joyce should choose as his signature Dubliner a Jew whose father converted to Protestantism and who himself converted to Catholicism in order to marry Molly, and someone whose love life with his wife has been upside-down since their young son's death eleven days after he was born. Nothing is resolved here about the Famine; Bloom's "report" is a pastiche of popular legend and lore, but the point has more to do with the paucity of structured knowledge about Irish history in Dublin at the turn of the century. However perceived, the Famine remains the most profound and consequential point of reference for any Irishman after 1845.

Both Joyce and Beckett needed to leave Ireland to write as Irishmen. As Terry Eagleton put it in *Heathcliff and the Great Hunger*, "the art of Samuel Beckett, with its starved landscapes that are at once Ireland and anywhere, shows well enough how to be stripped of your particular culture is to become a citizen of the world" (281-2) **[Figure 10]**. Beckett's venue is the stage instead of the page, and his exile allowed him to view his homeland as acutely as Joyce did his home city of Dublin. In a stage world as aphasic as Beckett's, staging becomes the key mode of communication. In *Happy Days* (1961), for example, the burial of the two main characters, Winnie and Willie, mixes images of graves for the living dead with the failed potato drills that led to such devastation when the crops failed in 1845. Language, as both Eagleton and Morash explain, is the mode of making meaning best suited to culture and civilization, and it is language that is either missing altogether (*Act Without Words*) or mangled and incomplete (*Krapp's Last Tape*) in Beckett. We sit before a sparsely populated stage listening to scraps of recorded conversation or in silence, watching the tilted movements of a mime on stage as we try to find sense. And, of course, meaning is difficult to come by since the main element of the narrative lies outside it: the Famine. Near the end of the third novel in Beckett's trilogy, *The Unnameable* (1953),

**Figure 10** | Louis le Brocquy, *Image of Samuel Beckett*

the narrative voice says, "It will be I? It will be the silence, where I am? I don't know, I'll never know: in the silence you don't know" (414). And that, of course, is the point of this modernist discourse around the Famine: "in the silence [about the Famine] you don't know" – about history, about life, about the future – and are suspended between ages, between tongues, between identities in permanent exile.

Joyce died in Zurich in January, 1941 and he is buried there; Yeats died in France in January 1939 and his remains were repatriated to Sligo in 1948; the younger Beckett died in France in 1989 and is buried there. By the time that generation of Irish modernists had passed away, the situation in Ireland had shifted into what Colm Toibín calls a period of "erasure," a reflection of the political climate after 1922. In the first half of the twentieth century, the most significant literary texts that addressed the legacy of the Famine were Liam O'Flaherty's 1937 novel *Famine* and Patrick Kavanagh's 1942 poem "The Great Hunger."

It would be fair to characterize *Famine*'s approach as sociological: the Famine of the 1840s reflects the fateful meeting between rural, timeless communities in western Ireland and the corrupted landowning classes, supported by the distant colonial government responsible for providing relief to those rural communities.

The community of the Kilmartins depends on the women who guide the rituals associated with birth and death, and the Famine emptied those rituals of meaning and traumatized the community. The slow but inexorable destruction of the community and of those dependent upon it seems almost Darwinian: inevitable, impersonal and final. The novel ends with Brian Kilmartin trying to bury the last of his family in the frozen ground: no one is left in the Black Valley and the few survivors are on ships bound for an uncertain future in the new world. "He clutched the handle of the spade, leaned forward, threatened the frosty earth with the point, and raised his foot. There was a deep, gurgling sound in his throat and he fell forward headlong" (448). We get the sense of a chapter in Irish life closing forever, "where the boundary between worlds (past, present, or future) is crossed" (McClean 142). This sense of the sun setting on a particular way of life associated with the Famine is also evoked by George "*AE*" Russell's painting *The Potato Gatherers* (1878)**[Figure 11]**. The two female figures in the foreground hurry to finish their work before the setting of the sun directly behind them and the approach of dusk.

Colm Toibín and Diarmaid Ferriter have argued that Kavanagh's "The Great Hunger" (1942) is "much more concerned with the contemporary world, with the spiritual and emotional famine" of his own time rather than with the Great Hunger

**Figure 11** | George 'AE' Russell, *The Potato Gatherers*

of 1845 (28). This reading of Kavanagh's poem (and Tom Murphy's later play *Famine*) suggests that we have moved into another iteration of post-Famine writing. In a sense, these two texts have more in common with Carleton's metaphoric framing of the Famine as representing the long-standing suffering of the rural Irish than with either the Gothic or modernist responses to the Famine. Here too there is a slow, inexorable grinding down of the main persona – the small farmer Patrick Maguire – from the travails of the rural agricultural life. The story is unsentimental (unlike the romanticization of this population by the writers of the Literary Revival), and the result is emotional isolation and alienation:

> *The graveyard in which he will lie will be just a deep-drilled*
> *potato field*
> *Where the seed gets no chance to come through*
> *To the fun of the sun.*
> *The tongue in his mouth is the root of a yew.*
> *Silence, silence. The story is done* (xiv, 68-73).

In this reading, the Famine – called "The Great Hunger" here for the first time – is a measure, a comparative metric meant to bring meaning to abstract notions such as the emotional desolation that crushing work brings to the peasant. The events of 1845-52 have thus fused into a far-reaching event against which other kinds of devastation can be measured.

About one hundred years after the coming of the potato blight to Ireland, Taoiseach Eamon de Valera, American-born but raised in Co. Clare, called for a long-overdue historical examination of the event and its consequences. The effort was to be led by Robert Dudley Edwards of University College Dublin, and would produce roughly a thousand pages of edited material to be published sometime in 1946. The result was disappointing, even to de Valera. The long-delayed work finally reached public view in 1956, with 436 pages of carefully measured and edited text under the title *The Great Famine: Studies in Irish History, 1845-52*. Perhaps the editor and the contributors sensed the political charge that the Famine carried after one hundred years of "erasure," but great care was taken not to assign responsibility for the million-plus deaths and nearly double that number of emigrants. The result was enough, though, to inaugurate what might be called the historical period of response to the Famine.

The rising tide of Irish nationalism after independence and partition solidified England's position as the villain in this narrative – much as John Mitchel had insisted a hundred years earlier – and the key question shifted from "What is the significance of the Famine?" to "To what uses can the Famine be put?" Eminent historian Christine Kinealy refers to this trend as "a heroic but simplistic view of Irish history" (n. pag.). The tepid neutrality of the Edwards volume now gave way to more muscular narratives that pushed the plot of these events toward one political position or another. One of the most contentious entries was written by Cecil Woodham-Smith: *The Great Hunger* (1962), which still elicits strong opinions, pro and con, among historians. No one, however, disputes the power of the narrative or the research that supports it. Part of this power comes from Woodham-Smith's clear-eyed sense for where responsibility for those tragic events lay: with Charles Trevelyan, the Assistant Secretary to the Treasury, as well as the long colonial antagonism between the two nations. As a well-respected biographer, Woodham-Smith had a knack for representing personalities as the key drivers of events. She could marshal powerful evidence to drive the narrative:

*The bones of the frame were covered with something which was skin but had a peculiar appearance, rough and dry like parchment, and hung in folds; eyes had sunk back into the head, the shoulder-bones were so high that the neck seemed to have sunk into the chest; face and neck were so wasted as to look like a skull; hair was thin, and there was an extraordinary pallor such as he [Sidney Godolphin Osborne] had never seen before (195).*

Here was the counterpoint to the impersonal academic historiographies written mid-century.

The book met with considerable resistance from the historical community, and when it received praise, it was always tempered with reservations about Woodham-Smith's academic qualifications, her gender, nationality, and/or methodology. Christine Kinealy notes that well-known historian Roy Foster "pejoratively described Woodham-Smith as 'a zealous convert', while, in 1964, a question in an undergraduate history examination paper in University College Dublin stated '*The Great Hunger* is a great novel. Discuss'"(n. pag.). The politics about representing the Famine seemed to have overshadowed any serious attempt to explore those terrible years and their impact on the most vulnerable citizens of the colony, at least among Irish historians.

One of the key differences between earlier famines and the 1845 Famine was American participation – both in terms of relief efforts and journalistic reporting on the devastation for an interested (and partisan) Irish immigrant population. Before 1840, this population had been mostly Protestant, and numbered somewhere between 450,000 and 600,000. Between 1830 and 1914, upwards of five million Irish emigrants came to American shores, most of them Catholic. The events of the Famine would be closely remembered in Irish-American communities, and as their political fortunes rose, those communities became sympathetic to the developing politics in Ireland as the nation moved closer to civil war and eventual independence. Irish-American communities contributed to relief efforts, and significant numbers of American Quakers went to the most stricken portions of Ireland to bring succor and relief. While initial responses in American newspapers often followed the Protestant Providentialist explanations circulated in English newspapers, once the scale of the devastation and the paucity of English relief efforts became widely known, the narrative shifted to blame English administrators for the death and sufferings, and extol the virtues of charity for these relatives across the ocean.[6] For Americans of Irish descent, the Famine was experienced through the sense of loss in those who went through forced emigration, and anger against the English politicians deemed responsible for the devastation.

These sentiments are powerfully evident in the work of one of Ireland's most prominent poets, Eavan Boland. Born in Dublin, Boland moved with her family to London and returned to Ireland to be educated. In *Outside History* (1990), the experiences of emigration, exile and isolation tie the Irish emigrant experience to the experience of being a woman, something that aligns well with what critic Margaret Kelleher discusses in her book, *The Feminization of the Famine* (1997). The suffering of women, Kelleher argues, is the key vector in Famine narratives, constituting a text within a text upon which the cultural meaning of the Famine can be written: "The female figure, as scene of hunger and 'bearer of meaning', receives a detailed physical inspection, never matched in characterizations of male famine victims" (24). These cultural markers resonate with maternity, sexuality, taboos and other symbolic loci that are part of the female image in Irish/Western society.

In Boland's "Mise Éire," this reads directly into the emigrant experience:

> *I am the woman*
>
> *in the gansy-coat*
>
> *on board the Mary Belle,*
>
> *in the huddling cold,*
>
> *holding her half dead baby to her*
>
> *as the wind shifts east*
>
> *and north over the dirty*
>
> *water of the wharf*
>
> *mingling the immigrant*
>
> *guttural with the vowels*
>
> *of homesickness who neither*
>
> *knows nor cares that*
>
> *a new language*
>
> *is a kind of scar*
>
> *and heals after a while*
>
> *into a passable imitation*
>
> *of what went before* (28-44).

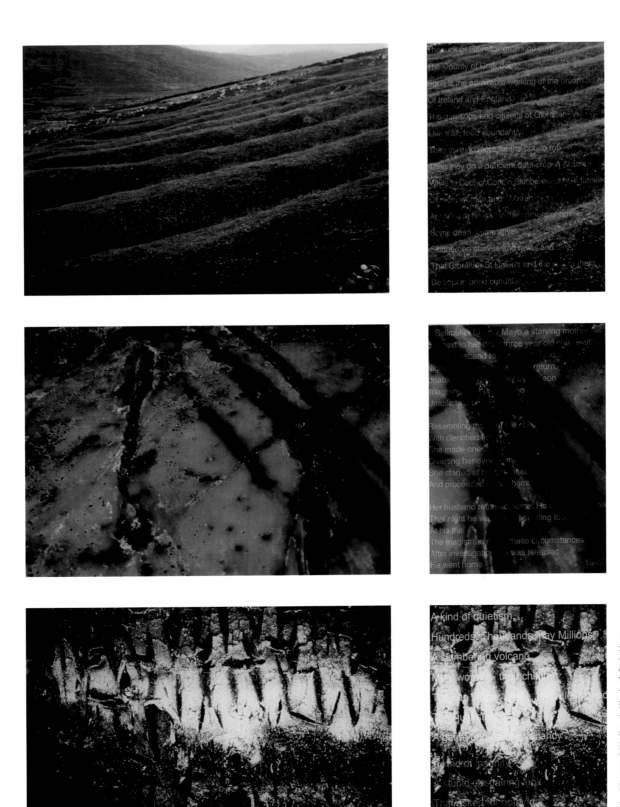

**Figure 12** | Alanna O'Kelly, *A Kind of Quietism*

In another poem, "That The Science of Cartography is Limited," the contemporary is overshadowed by the history buried in the landscape of Ireland, as the persona of the poem recalls her discovery that the ground that she and her partner stand upon in Connacht was once a Famine road:

> *Where they died, there the road ended*
> *and ends still and when I take down*
> *the map of this island, it is never so*
> *I can say here is*
> *the masterful, the apt rendering of*
> *the spherical as flat, nor*
> *an ingenious design which persuades a curve*
> *into a plane,*
> *but to tell myself again that*
> *the line which says woodland and cries hunger*
> *and gives out among sweet pine and cypress,*
> *and finds no horizon*
> *will not be there* (16–29).

There are two maps here: the familiar one we would consult for direction, and then there is the map that lies outside the science of cartography, a map of suffering that lies buried in the land, always. Alanna O'Kelly's work *A Kind of Quietism* (1990), from Ireland's Great Hunger Museum, resonates with the argument that an Irish landscape post-Famine is best read as a "map of suffering": the three layers in the photographic collage reveal that beneath the iconic green surface of the west of Ireland lie Famine roads, graves, wounds upon the land wrought by the events of 1845–52 **[Figure 12]**. Cultural eclipse – when the past occludes the present – is typical of the most effective modern responses to the Famine, where the present, the immediate is suddenly eclipsed by those memories of the Famine which lay shrouded in silence for nearly a century.

For other literary "exiles" in the twentieth century, the Famine experience transcends politics – including the politics of partition. Seamus Heaney, born in Northern Ireland and a founding member of the Field Day Group, was interested in working beyond the political fences that represented the antagonisms between Northern Ireland and the Republic of Ireland, and his first major collection of poems, *Death of a Naturalist* (1991), reflects that aim. Perhaps the best example of this occurs in "At a Potato Digging": the poem refers to the "famine god" who, even in the era of mechanical diggers, must be appeased by the humans dependent on the tuber for their welfare:

*Live skulls, blind-eyed, balanced on*

*wild higgledy skeletons*

*scoured the land in "forty-five,"*

*wolfed the blighted root and died.*

*The new potato, sound as stone,*

*putrefied when it had lain*

*three days in the long clay pit.*

*Millions rotted along with it.*

*Mouths tightened in, eyes died hard,*

*faces chilled to a plucked bird.*

*In a million wicker huts*

*beaks of famine snipped at guts.*

*A people hungering from birth,*

*grubbling, like plants, in the bitch earth,*

*were grafted with a great sorrow.*

*Hope rotted like a marrow.*

*Stinking potatoes fouled the land,*

*pits turned pus into filthy mounds:*

*and where potato diggers are*

*you still smell the running sore* (iii, 29-46).

Everything in this simple rural scene is redolent of a previous, tragic age in which death, suffering and eviction attended the "flint-white, purple" potato. The past, *this* past is always attendant upon the present. Past and present in a way comprise a nearly seamless passageway, where being *here* is also being *then and there*. In this formulation there is no past, really, just a many-dimensioned present within which the silent souls of the nineteenth century populate the landscapes of the present.

In his contribution to the monumental *Atlas of the Great Irish Famine* (2012), Chris Morash deftly summarizes the problem that anyone writing about the Famine has to address:

*the Famine challenges the limits and possibilities of literary representation, so that the subject of any Famine text is the search for an adequate form of representation. By the same token, the subject of any Famine text is the related (but by no means identical) search for an interpretative context in which death on a massive scale might make some kind of sense* (645).

Almost any sort of representation diminishes the scope of suffering in order to provide comprehension; it also changes the event – irretrievably – into something other than what those million-plus victims and their survivors experienced. Inevitably, the first works about the Famine produced during the Famine were already post-Famine. They were cultural constructions dislodged from the actualities on the ground. This aesthetic displacement led to an alignment of Famine writing with other cultural registers like politics, and many writers, new and old, have defaulted to relegating the horrors of the Famine to the background of what are actually common, even clichéd literary plots. More provocative examples of Famine writing reach for more complex and difficult-to-resolve narratives. Compare, for example, Brendan Graham's 1999 novel *The Whitest Flower* with Joseph O'Connor's 2002 *Star of the Sea*. *The Whitest Flower* is a typical romance story which could be deployed against a number of traumatic backgrounds, while O'Connor's novel struggles against the conventionalizing power of the novel form.

*Star of the Sea* is a nuanced book that avoids many of the more clichéd romance details by adopting a different manner of deploying historical evidence in the story. As Terry Eagleton (a fan of the novel) explains in his review, "The book is a montage of verbal forms: letters, quotation, first-person narrative, Hansard, captain's log, snatches of ballad, advertisements, news-paper clippings, historical documentation." This is precisely how Bram Stoker told his story about the colonizing vampire from the East: the atomizing of the central narrative authority so characteristic of the Victorian realist novel not only preserved a space for elements of the Famine to find their way into the story, but it also featured an Irish female persona as the chief narrative hand of the novel. This proves to be key in *Dracula*, as it does in *Star of the Sea*, which manages to bring the contrasts between the impoverished peasantry and the segregated upper classes into sharp focus in the characters' journey to the new world.

Absence, erasures, displacements: these are the common aspects of post-Famine writing that cross all modes of representation. Violence, according to Tom Murphy, is another consequence of the Famine, along with other kinds of cultural and national impoverishment:

*A hungry and demoralized people becomes silent, people emigrate in great numbers and leave spaces that cannot be filled. Intelligence becomes cunning. There is a poverty of thought and expression. Womanhood becomes harsh. Love, tenderness, loyalty, generosity go out the door in the struggle for survival. Men fester in vicarious dreams of destruction* (xi).

These consequences exist *sub rosa* in modern writing about the Famine, and by the time we reach Murphy's landmark production of *Famine* (1968), the historical setting for the story of John Connor, his family, and community becomes translucent: it concerns the present as much as 1846-7, something Murphy himself acknowledges: "while aware of the public event that was the Irish Famine in the 1840s, I was drawing on the private well and recreating moods and events, apprehensions of myself and my own times" (xiv). The publication of *Famine* together with two other consciously political plays shows his use of the Famine and the powerful, tragic story of John Connor to reframe the present using the past, as though Irish history restarted after the Famine, making everything that follows a consequence of the Famine.

Connor's Job-like passivity reflects the present as much as it reimagines affairs in the rural west of Ireland in 1846. This is a point made by Colm Tóibín, mentioned previously: "Patrick Kavanagh's long poem 'The Great Hunger' (1942) and Tom Murphy's play *Famine* (1968), are much more concerned with the contemporary world, with the spiritual and emotional famine of their own times" ("Erasures" 17). An existential desolation followed the Famine and pervades the country in the twentieth and twenty-first centuries. One is tempted to argue that from 1845 to the present, the Famine has been one event unfolding over several acts. In a 2010 op-ed in the *New York Times*, Nobel-winning economist Paul Krugman tied Ireland's recent economic woes to the period of the Famine, as though the Irish were once again experiencing the consequences of economic decisions made in the capitals of the UK.

The same is true of Murphy's best-known colleague in the theatre, Brian Friel, in *Translations* (1980). The play is set in 1833 in a small Donegal community as the arrival of the British Ordnance Survey starts the steep decline of the Irish language and culture, a decline accelerated by the Famine of 1845. Friel has staged a conundrum, however, that all post-Famine literature shares: Donegal in 1833 cannot be imagined or staged after 1845 – it's no longer accessible. All such conflicts between British authorities, between a native Irish culture and the world brought in via the English language, have become post-Famine phenomena. This becomes clear in the play once the fields and homes of the village have been destroyed. Young Bridget – confused and distraught because of the destruction – suddenly wheels around, sniffs the air and says, "The sweet smell! Smell it! Jesus, it's the potato blight!" (83). Friel – a charter member, with Stephen Rea, of the Field Day theatre company – chose to produce *Translations* for the first time at the Guildhall, Derry, Northern Ireland on September 23, 1980. It's fair to suggest that Friel – despite his claims that *Translations* is unpolitical – staged the play to transcend post-partition politics. Unlike previous famines, the Famine of 1845 was politically charged almost immediately, something intimated by Carleton's Preface to *The Black Prophet*, and this political charge has not diminished in the 170 years since.

As the work of Murphy and Friel suggests, one of the most vital strains of post-Famine writing has been for the stage, from Hubert O'Grady (*Famine*, 1886) to Synge's Abbey Theatre experiments with W. B. Yeats, through Sean O'Casey's political plays of the 1920s, to Beckett's sparse theatre of the 1950s. The immediacy of the stage allows writers to explore the transcendent power and draw of the Famine and its horrors; Irish theatre has revisited the Famine in nearly every generation since the end of the nineteenth century. Two of the most innovative recent dramatists – Conor McPherson and Marina Carr – have also revisited the Gothic legacy of the Famine in two of the most provocative plays of the last twenty years, *The Weir* (1997) by McPherson and *By the Bog of Cats* (1998) by Carr. *The Weir* is a ghost story; the characters are haunted by ghosts and the action culminates in a round of storytelling which details their desolation. Where storytelling had once defined and strengthened the community, these stories explain how the ghostly tracks of the dead sabotage meaningful personal connections. McPherson explains in an interview:

*I think probably all the kind of things in your life that are unresolved [...] have to be compacted in order to find some resolution, but in a way they have to exist in a sort of spiritual place [...] In any ghost story, ghosts come back because there's some sort of unfinished business. And I think it's about that: the [...] existential unfinished business* (Grobe 566).

With that last reference to "existential unfinished business," McPherson stands with other post-Famine writers who have mapped the consequences of that terrible chapter in Irish history. At the end of *The Weir*, after Valerie – the mysterious newcomer from Dublin – has told her tale of being haunted by her dead daughter, the congregants in the pub complain about German tourists and then depart with nothing but their existential loneliness. All that is left to do is turn off the lights and leave.

Carr's *By the Bog of Cats* is a trenchant retelling of Euripides' *Medea* within an Irish context, reaching back to a story about a terrifying, desperate revenge by a foreign woman in response to the perfidies of her adopted countrymen. In Carr's retelling, the focus is on Hester Swane, a member of the Traveling community who struggles to connect with her missing mother Josie Swane – a local drinking and singing legend – and worries about the loss of her daughter Josie to the child's father. The centrality of the mother is part of the Famine resonance of the play, something noted by Cathy Leeney: "In this way the play is radical in the Irish canon. It is an enactment of mourning for the absent mother; this is not only Hester's mother, but theatrically speaking, the mother absent from so many important Irish plays" (160). Carr's focus on the absent or dead mother presents the other side of Margaret Kelleher's argument in *The Feminization of Famine*, that the traditional depiction of female victims in Famine imagery constitutes a text in and of itself, one connected to the typical representation of Ireland as female. Carr's play is "haunted, literally and figuratively, by the dead, by suicide or killing, by the act of dying" (Leeney 158). Unlike Murphy's *Famine*, however, these women die by their own hands, not at the hands of their husbands. The central symbol of the play is the black swan, and when we first encounter the dead swan being dragged across a bloody trail in the snow, we understand that events are locked toward tragedy and will not be diverted: "Hester – She's gone – Hester – She's cut her heart out – it's lyin' there on top of her chest like some dark feathered bird" (396).

In a 2012 article about Patrick McCabe and his brand of "bog Gothic," Ellen Scheible notes that in the Gothic, "the human body trumps all other symbols" as a representation "for the inherent paradox underlying national identity" (5). Is there an historical event in which the body – dead, decayed, dismembered, remembered, disappeared, absent – has been more prominently at the center of meaning than in the Great Irish Famine? The Famine becomes Gothic when the predominant image from all the reporting on both sides of the Atlantic and beyond is the ravaged human body, the destroyed human body, the missing human body, and its attendant coffins and mass graves. Thus, post-Famine, absent bodies, ghostly revenants, and emptied human habitations are always Famine references in Irish literature. So are doubled identities in conflict with each other, paralleled planes of existence – past and present – and dead children and mothers. One of the most striking examples of this ghostly aesthetic is the work of Patrick McCabe, especially his creepiest book to date, *Winterwood* **[Figure 13]**.

The main character is Redmond Hatch, a journalist enjoying the benefits of the Celtic Tiger economy, who leaves the comforts of Dublin to visit his childhood home (Slievenageeha) about which he has fond, if incomplete memories. The man he has come to see, the backwoods Pan figure Ned Strange, is a liminal figure, someone rooted in Redmond's muddled past, while he is highlighted in Redmond's writing as a figure in the cultural margins of contemporary Ireland. The Gothic, however, does not acknowledge modernity or the future – these are chimera that explode in the collision with the dimly limned past. This is Redmond's discovery: after Ned is implicated in the terrible murder of a young boy (an analog for Redmond as a child), Redmond writes, "A place – as has so often been observed about such places – where the inhabitants never looked you in the eye, where everything they did seemed sly and calculated. It was as if everything they represented was to be found in him" (43). Both Slievenageeha and Dublin have become suspect terrain as Redmond's memory and his reconstructed narrative become doubtful and sinister. Past becomes inseparable from present, and Ned's role as the narrator of Redmond's abusive family history drives Redmond into an epistemological madness where truth and fiction are inseparable. He is divorced and separated from his wife and daughter, reinvents himself as a filmmaker, and after Ned's suicide, is haunted by the old man who becomes the driver for the horrible crimes that Redmond commits against his estranged family.

"Winterwood" is Redmond's word for the place where he has buried his daughter and his ex-wife, to which he returns periodically to engage in in some sort of meditation with them. It recalls "Black '47", where the dead lie planted in the frozen ground, where men like John Connor in *Famine* have consigned the bodies of their doomed families to lie nameless, bodiless in time. The power of the Gothic comes from its persistent transgressions: of time, blending past and present until neither is completely discernible; of place, so that centuries-old landscapes colonize the modern places we live in; and of meaning, so that the "past-ness" of things is always debatable, always unsure, and at any moment might break through the flimsy accommodations we call modern life to insist that the past is never gone, never fully buried, never ameliorated. These elements of the Gothic have given the genre a flexible register of meaning that can be adapted to any age or place without eliding the insistent presence of the nameless dead, the disappeared families and emptied villages from the 1845 Famine. That is why it has persisted to the present day, and why we might say that it haunts all Irish literature post-Famine.

Figure 13 | Sam Weber, *Winterwood*

# CONCLUSION

Few literatures draw so profoundly from an historical event as Irish literature does from the Great Famine. Why, we could ask, has this literature hewed so strongly toward the modernist mode or the Gothic register, and why has it so often found meaning in its attachment to other discourses such as politics? In Trollope's *Castle Richmond*, for example, the events from the second half of the 1840s in Ireland are not problematic at all: they make sense within the larger narrative scaffolding of the all-encompassing realistic novel as practiced by Victorian novelists. And that, of course, is the problem addressed by the works discussed in this essay. Let me return for a moment to Eagleton's *Heathcliff and The Great Irish Famine* for some clues about why this is so. In addressing the reasons why it "thrived less robustly in Ireland than in Britain," Eagleton explains that the "realist novel is the form par excellence of settlement and stability, gathering individual lives into an integrated whole; and social conditions in Ireland hardly lent themselves to any such sanguine reconciliation" (147). English readers assumed "that the world is story-shaped – that there is a well-formed narrative implicit in reality itself, which it is the task of such realism to represent" (147). That was not true for Irish writers and readers – certainly after 1845 and perhaps even earlier as a result of the colonial oppositions that had been part of Ireland's vexed relationship with the English language since the seventeenth century. This is the argument of Jarlath Killeen in *Gothic Ireland: Horror and the Irish Anglican Imagination in the Long Eighteenth Century* (2005), who sees in this indeterminacy the source waters for the Irish Gothic tradition:

*Gothic is the national form, as cultural hybridity lies at the centre […] This specifically Irish text is the epic of the Irish nation because it refuses the "reconciliation of opposites" associated with the novel form, a reconciliation that is really just the celebration of the ideological hegemony of the powerful* (222).

The Famine of 1845 is in large part attributable to this "ideological hegemony of the powerful," evident both in the long-standing inequities between the two nations and in the failed relief strategies of the Russell government. The politicization of Irish literature, its adoption of a Gothic register as the "national form," and the modernist

experiment with English forms and language were the means available to Irish writers attempting to represent the horrors of the Famine, and they have become the distinctive elements of post-Famine Irish writing. It is this development that I have traced in this essay. Metaphorically, I meant this study to operate more like a map than a catalog: the writers and texts discussed here attempted to emerge from under the pall of 1845–52, some more successfully than others, but, as I argue, in an effort to explore how "Irishness" had been affected by the Famine. Without doubt, this effort is not yet completed and new and different iterations of what Seamus Deane termed "the question of what the Famine meant" will be written, staged, and filmed as we approach the 175th anniversary of the visitation of the potato blight to Ireland.

# ENDNOTES

[1] Critics refer to this debate as the constructivist (meaning is brought to the text) as opposed to objectivist (meaning is in the text) argument. Perhaps the best known participant in these debates is Stanley Fish, whose Is *There a Text in This Class?* is influential.

[2] The title of this essay is taken from William Carleton's *The Black Prophet*: "The roads were literally black with funerals, and as you passed along from parish to parish, the death-bells were pealing forth, in slow but dismal tones, the gloomy triumph which pestilence was achieving over the face of our devoted country – a country that each successive day filled with darker desolation and deeper mourning" (150).

[3] The Gothic lexicon was actually quite common by the turn of the nineteenth century in Irish Republican politics, in Wolfe Tone's work for example. See Smart and Hutcheson.

[4] "The conditions of colonised Ireland could not readily be accommodated within the canonical British forms of representation such as the realist novel" (Whelan 63-64.) This point was also made by Terry Eagleton in *Heathcliff and the Great Hunger*.

[5] "Ireland is the fatigue-ground of English imagination," wrote the *Nation* in 1848; "Mrs. Radcliffe being dead [...] it is now our part to furnish England with monsters, thugs, and 'devils great and devils small'" (Morash 116).

[6] See Farrell.

# WORKS CITED

Beckett, Samuel. *Three Novels by Samuel Beckett: Malloy, Malone Dies, The Unnamable.* New York: Grove Press, 1958.

Boland, Eavan. *"Mise Éire."Outside History: Selected Poems 1980–1990.* New York: Norton, 1990. 79.

---. "That The Science of Cartography is Limited." *Outside History.* 2.

Carleton, William. *The Black Prophet: A Tale of Irish Famine.* London, Belfast: Simms & McIntyre, 1848.

Carr, Marina. *By the Bog of Cats. Modern and Contemporary Irish Drama.* Ed. John P. Harrington. New York: W. W. Norton & Company, 2009. 563-567.

Crowley, John, William J. Smyth, and Mike Murphy, eds. *Atlas of the Great Irish Famine.* Cork: Cork UP, 2012.

Deane, Seamus. *Strange Country: Modernity and Nationhood in Irish Writing since 1790.* Oxford: Clarendon Press, 1997.

---. "Dumbness and Eloquence: A Note on English as We Write It in Ireland." *Ireland and Postcolonial Theory.* Ed. Clare Carroll and Patricia King. Notre Dame: University of Notre Dame Press, 2003. 109-128.

Eagleton, Terry. *Heathcliff and The Great Hunger.* London: Verso, 1995.

---. "Another country." Review of *Star of the Sea* by Joseph O'Connor. *Guardian* 25 January 2003. Online.

Edwards, R. D. and T. D. Williams (eds.). *The Great Famine: Studies in Irish History, 1845-52.* New York: New York UP, 1957.

Egan, Charles. *The Killing Snows.* Bristol: SilverWood Books, 2012.

Farrell, James M. "Reporting the Irish Famine in America: Images of "Suffering Ireland" in the American Press, 1845-1848." *Communication Scholarship* (2014), Paper 17.

Fish, Stanley. *Is There a Text in This Class? The Authority of Interpretative Communities.* Cambridge, MA: Harvard UP, 1980.

Friel, Brian. *Translations.* London: Faber and Faber, 1981.

Gibbons, Luke. *Gaelic Gothic: Race, Colonization, and Irish Culture.* Galway: Arlen House, 2004.

---. *Limits of the Visible: Representing the Great Hunger.* Hamden, CT: Quinnipiac UP/Ireland's Great Hunger Museum, 2014.

Grobe, Christopher A. "Secular Morality in the Plays of Conor McPherson." *Modern and Contemporary Irish Drama.* Ed. John P. Harrington. New York: Norton, 2009. 563-567.

Heaney, Seamus. "At a Potato Digging." *Death of a Naturalist.* London: Faber and Faber, 1966. 31-33.

Joyce, James. *Ulysses.* New York: Vintage, 1990.

---. *Dubliners.* New York: Penguin/Viking Books, 1996.

Kavanagh, Patrick. "The Great Hunger." *The Complete Poems.* Newbridge, Kildare: Goldsmith, 1992. 104.

Kelleher, Margaret. *The Feminization of Famine.* Durham: Duke UP, 1997.

Killeen, Jarlath. *Gothic Ireland: Horror and the Irish Anglican Imagination in the Long Eighteenth Century.* Dublin: Four Courts, 2005.

Kinealy, Christine. "Beyond Revisionism: reassessing The Great Irish Famine." *History Ireland.* 3.4 (Winter 1995). Web. 20 April 2015.

Krugman, Paul. "Eating The Irish." *New York Times* 26 November 2010: A2.

Leeney, Cathy. "Ireland's 'exiled' women playwrights: Teresa Deevy and Marina Carr." *The Cambridge Companion to Twentieth-Century Irish Drama*. Cambridge: Cambridge UP, 2004. 150-163.

Mangan, Clarence. *The Autobiography of James Clarence Mangan*. Ed James Kilroy. Dublin: Dolmen, 1968.

---. "The Nameless One." *His Collected Poems*. Norwood, MA: Norwood Press, 1897. (Cornel University Library Reprint). 341.

McCabe, Patrick. *Winterwood: A Novel*. London: Bloomsbury, 2006.

McClean, Stuart. *The Event and Its Terrors: Ireland, Famine, Modernity*. Stanford: Stanford UP, 2004.

McPherson, Conor. *The Weir. Modern and Contemporary Irish Drama*. Ed. John P. Harrington. New York: Norton, 2009. 309-351.

Mitchel, John. *Jail Journal*. London: Sphere Books, 1983.

Morash, Chris. *Writing the Irish Famine*. Oxford: Oxford UP, 1995.

Murphy, Tom. *Plays: One (Famine, The Patriot Game, The Blue Macushla)*. London: Methuen Drama, 1992.

O'Connor, Joseph. *Star of the Sea*. New York: Harcourt, 2002.

O'Flaherty, Liam. *Famine*. Boston: David R. Godine Publishers, 1982.

Ó Gráda, Cormac and Diarmaid Ó Muirithe, "The Famine of 1740-41: Representations in Gaelic Poetry." *Éire-Ireland* 45.3&4 (Fomhar/Geimhreadh / Fall/Winter 2010): 41-62.

Ryan, Alan. *Cast a Cold Eye*. New York: Tom Doherty Associates Books, 1999.

Scheible, Ellen. *Reanimating the Nation: Patrick McCabe, Neil Jordan, and the Bog Gothic*. Bridgewater Review 31.1 (2012): 4-6.

Smart, Robert A. and Michael R. Hutcheson. "'The Unborn and Unburied Dead': The Rhetoric of Ireland's *An Gorta Mór*." *Ireland's Great Hunger: Silence, Memory and Commemoration*. Ed. Christine Kinealy and David Valone. New York: University Press of America, 2003. 65-83.

Stoker, Bram. *Dracula*. New York: Modern Library, 1996.

Thompson, G. Richard. *Romantic Gothic Tales, 1790-1810*. New York: Harper & Row, 1979.

Toibín, Colm. "Erasures: Colm Toibín on the Great Irish Famine." *London Review of Books* 20.15 (30 July 1998): 17-23.

---. and Diarmaid Ferriter. *The Irish Famine: a Documentary*. London: Profile Books, 1999.

Trollope, Anthony. *Castle Richmond*. Oxford: Oxford UP, 1992.

Whelan, Kevin. "The Memories of 'The Dead.'" *Yale Journal of Criticism* 15.1 (Spring 2002): 59-97.

Woodham-Smith, Cecil. *The Great Hunger: Ireland 1845-1849*. London: Penguin, 1962.

Yeats, W. B. *Countess Cathleen*. Project Gutenburg. Web. 8 July 2015.

ROBERT SMART

# IMAGES

**Cover**

Robert Ballagh
b. 1943
*An Gorta Mór*
2012
Stained glass window
58.5 x 58.5 in (148.6 x 148.6 cm)
© Robert Ballagh
Image courtesy of Ireland's
Great Hunger Museum,
Quinnipiac University

**Figure 1**

Daniel Macdonald
1821-1853
*An Irish Peasant Family
Discovering the Blight of their
Store*
1847
Oil on canvas
33 x 41 in (83.8 x 104 cm)
National Folklore Collection,
University College Dublin

**Figure 2**

James Mahony
"The Hut or Watch-House in
the Old Chapel Yard" [Detail]
*The Illustrated London News*
February 12, 1847

**Figure 3**

Frederic William Burton
1816-1900
*James Clarence Mangan
(1803-1849), Poet, after his
Death in the Meath Hospital,
Dublin, 1849*
1849
Black and red chalk on paper
11.5 x 14.9 in (29.3 x 37.8 cm)
© National Gallery of Ireland

**Figure 4**

Jock McFadyen
b. 1950
*Irish Gothic*
1987
Oil on canvas
81.5 x 83.5 in (207 x 212 cm)
©Jock McFadyen
Image courtesy of Wolverhampton
Art Gallery

**Figure 5**

Robert Seymour
1798-1836
*Two Species of Irish Vampire*
*The Looking Glass*
1831
Lithograph on paper
16 x 11 in (40.6 x 28 cm)
Image courtesy of The Victoria
and Albert Museum

**Figure 6**

John D. Reigh
c. 1875 – 1914
"Ireland Wrestles with Famine
While Mr. Balfour Plays Golf"
*United Ireland*
August 23, 1890
10.7 x 15.4 in (27.2 x 39.1 cm)
Image courtesy of The National
Library of Ireland

**Figure 7**

Harry Clarke (Irish, 1889–1931)
Clarke Studios, Dublin, maker
Detail of *"The Dreamers"*
by Lennox Robinson and
*"The Countess Cathleen"*
*by W. B. Yeats*, from stained
glass window, commissioned
1926, completed 1930
(never installed)
For the International Labor
Building, League of Nations,
Geneva
Stained glass, lead cames
71 1/2 x 40 In
(181.6 x 101.6 cm)
The Wolfsonian–Florida
International University,
Miami Beach, Florida,
The Mitchell Wolfson, Jr.
Collection
TD1988.34.1
Photo: Bruce White

**Figure 8**

John Butler Yeats
1839-1922
*Portrait of William Butler Yeats
(1865-1939), Poet*
1900
Oil on canvas
30.3 x 25.2 in (77 x 64 cm)
©National Gallery of Ireland

**Figure 9**

Jacques-Emile Blanche
1861-1942
*James Joyce*
1935
Oil on canvas
49.25 x 34.5 in (125 cm x 87.6 cm)
© National Portrait Gallery,
London

**Figure 10**

Louis le Brocquy
1916-2012
*Image of Samuel Beckett*
1979
Oil on canvas
31.5 x 31.5 in (80 x 80 cm)
(442)
© Estate of Louis le Brocquy

**Figure 11**

George William "AE" Russell
1867-1935
*The Potato Gatherers*
Oil on canvas
Reproduced with the kind
permission of Armagh County
Museum

**Figure 12**

Alanna O'Kelly
b. 1955
*A Kind of Quietism*
1990
Photo text
3 panels: 19.7 x 29.5 in
(50 x 75 cm)
3 panels: 19.7 x 16.6 in
(50 x 42 cm)
© Alanna O'Kelly
Image courtesy of Ireland's
Great Hunger Museum,
Quinnipiac University

**Figure 13**

Sam Weber
*Winterwood*
Cover of *Winterwood*,
novel by Patrick McCabe.
© Sam Weber

ROBERT SMART

# ABOUT THE AUTHOR

Robert Smart is the Dean of the College of Arts and Sciences and Professor of English at Quinnipiac University (Connecticut, USA), where he teaches advanced writing, Irish Studies, and Gothic Studies courses. Smart is the founding editor of *The Writing Teacher*, co-editor of *Direct From the Disciplines*, and author of *The Nonfiction Novel*. He has published on Irish Studies and Gothic Studies in several anthologies and in *Postcolonial Text*.

Quinnipiac University would like to thank the copyright holders
for granting permission to reproduce works illustrated in this book.
Every effort has been made to contact the holders of copyrighted
material. Omissions will be corrected in future editions if the
publisher is notified in writing.

All rights reserved. No part of this publication may be reproduced
or transmitted by any means, electronic or mechanical, including
photocopy, recording or any other storage and retrieval system,
without prior permission in writing from the publisher.

IRELAND'S GREAT HUNGER MUSEUM | QUINNIPIAC UNIVERSITY PRESS ©2015

**SERIES EDITORS**

Niamh O'Sullivan
Grace Brady

**IMAGE RESEARCH**

Claire Puzarne

**DESIGN**

Rachel Foley

**ACKNOWLEDGMENT**

Office of Public Affairs, Quinnipiac University

**PUBLISHER**

Quinnipiac University Press

**PRINTING**

GRAPHYCEMS

ISBN 978-0-9904686-4-6

**Ireland's Great Hunger** Museum
Quinnipiac University

3011 Whitney Avenue
Hamden, CT 06518-1908
203-582-6500

**www.ighm.org**